Satori

This small book describes the main steps of the Buddhist path that leads directly to understanding.
The path to truth and peace.

To my mother

Holger Junghardt

Satori

The path to understanding

Bibliographical Information of the Deutsche Nationalbibliothek

This publication is listed in the Deutsche Nationalbibliographie of the Deutsche Nationalbibliothek; detailed bibliographical information can be accessed under http: //dnb.d-nb.de

© 2022 Holger Junghardt
Printing, Production and Layout: BoD – Books on Demand
ISBN: 978-3-7557-7515-7

Table of contents

1 Introduction

"Satori" is a Japanese word and means "understanding".

The path to understanding was already taken 2,500 years ago and since then this teaching has been passed on until today. And therefore, in this booklet, I would like to call the man by name and pass on his insights as he once put them into words. This is Siddharta Gautama, more commonly known as the Buddha ("the Awakened One").

Even though the following pages are about Buddhism, the focus should always be on the description of the path. To begin this path, one must make oneself empty, have an open mind. Because ideas and concepts prevent the emergence of understanding.

To all those who do not succeed immediately, the following hints should help. In order to follow the Buddhist path, one does not have to give up one's own religion. For even though Buddhism is associated with the term religion, it is not a religion. Religions always consist of a belief system. Only if I believe in the one God/gods, then I will get further on my path. In addition, many church faith organizations operate on guilt and fear. Buddhism is just the opposite. For example, Buddha asked his disciples to constantly examine the teachings of his path instead of demanding blind obedience and faith. For either I believe something or I see the truth. A famous master (Bhagwan Shree Rajneesh) summed it up in one short sentence: "Anybody who gives you a belief system is your enemy".

Following the Buddhist path does not mean giving up one's

original religion with its beliefs. In Japan, Shintoism and Buddhism coexist in harmony. While Shintoism expresses connection with nature and ancestors (with a multitude of gods), Buddhism is concerned with death and burials. Shrines and temples stand side by side in peace. Also in this booklet will be the name of Jesus.

A Zen master once said: "Whenever I pronounce the name Buddha, I should go to the river and rinse my mouth three times". I will therefore present the teaching in such a way that it can be understood as independently as possible from the ideas and concepts of Buddhism. Should the reader find himself digressing from the contents of the teaching to ideas about Buddhism (Buddha figures, impressive temples, Far Eastern music, esotericism, religion, faith, etc.), our Zen master also has advice here, for one of his disciples replied: "Whenever I hear the name Buddha, I should go to the river and wash out my ears three times".

This book was written after more than 20 years of meditation and mindfulness practice, study of Buddhist literature, Dharma lectures and retreats with Thich Nhat Hanh, among others.

Originally, this book was a private summary. I would be very happy if it would be helpful to the reader as well.

At the end, some questions are answered in an unconventional way, which may possibly accelerate the process of understanding.

According to Master Linji, there is no need for too many words for realization, since all the facilities are already within oneself. The scope of this book wants to adhere to this specification.

2 The Four Noble Truths

Gautama Siddharta lived over 2,500 years ago as a rich and sheltered prince at a palace in northeast India. He led a life that most of us would wish for. He spent his childhood and youth in a paradisiacal palace. But on a journey he was confronted with sick and old people as well as death. These experiences marked him so deeply that he sought different ways of meditation to process these impressions.

During this time he recognized the "Four Noble Truths" and developed the "Noble Eightfold Path" with solutions.

2.1 1st Truth: life is suffering

Life is not perfect. Beautiful days are followed by hard times. Thirst, hunger, pain, diseases, fears, loss of beloved creatures can make life unbearable. No living being is free from these sufferings. The fear of these is latent even in good times. Ultimately, life ends with death, with which we will lose everything.

2.2 2nd Truth: causes of suffering

Attachment, greed, hatred, all delusions in general, are the cause of suffering. The idea of an independent and constant ego makes us suffer. We have ideas of how it should be and give concepts to all objects, which pretend an independence and own reality. If our notions are not realized, hatred sets in (against others or ourselves) and we fight against that which we believe is opposed to us. Delusions prevent the view of truth and reality.

2.3 3rd Truth: abolition of suffering

It is quite trivial: if the causes of suffering disappear (the Buddha called them unwholesome actions), suffering also disappears.

2.4 4th Truth: way to the abolition of suffering

The Buddha developed a way to avoid suffering. He called this the "Noble Eightfold Path". It consists of eight individual measures, which can be summarized into three groups.

First, the teaching must be recognized and understood (1. right view), and the decision (2. right thought) must be made to follow this path. However, this is not a half-hearted decision, but a radical decision to want to change one's life.

According to this fundamental decision, unwholesome actions are to be avoided. The Buddha referred here to speech (3. right speech), action (4. right action) and life acquisition (5. right livelihood). We will look at this in more detail below.

The third group seems to make the most abstract demands, but these are the most important: effort (6. right effort), mindfulness (7. right mindfulness) and collection (8. right concentration).

These three points in particular require a great deal of energy and stamina, but are essential to successfully follow the path. You have to fill your life with mindfulness at every moment and practice this state again and again. We will also take a detailed look at what this looks like exactly.

3 The Noble Eightfold Path

The Noble Eightfold Path is a pure instruction for action. First, it will be considered in detail. A discussion of the individual points will follow later.

3.1 The acceptance of the teaching: view and thought

Fortunately, in modern times it is easy to come into contact with Far Eastern philosophies even in Western countries. There are more and more Buddhist groups (Sanghas) that meet also outside of monasteries and where everybody can get to know the content of the teaching (Dharma).

The Buddha, the Dharma and the Sangha are also called the Three Jewels of Refuge.

Naturally, it will be easier to follow the Buddhist path for those who have a desire to do so, perhaps because they are currently in a crisis. But anyone can be helped by this teaching because it is the path to truth and can dissolve delusions. And as we will see later, this path is a direct path to peace. So I hope that my readers will take this path for themselves and perhaps accompany others.

3.2 Avoiding unwholesome actions: speech, action and livelihood

The three basic poisons delusion, greed and hatred are the causes of all suffering. They are found again in speech, action and the acquisition of life.

Actually, speech and action would already include life acquisition. But many people consider life acquisition separate from their other areas of life. There is no separation, but possibly this grouping is helpful for some people. For example, the Buddha was referring here to occupations that involve killing. A butcher does not necessarily kill for the pleasure of killing, but because it is his work, yet it is an unwholesome act.

There is a very beautiful Buddhist story about this. A young man was employed as a butcher. Every day he killed many animals as part of his work for the slaughterhouse. At one point, he looked into the eyes of a cow against which he was lifting the axe and realized that this cow had tears in its eyes. After this experience, he gave up his profession.

Greed and hatred are the most common motives for acts of killing. Basically, other living beings should not be killed or injured, because every living being wants to be happy. Humans could be feed very well on plant food and therefore would not need to kill animals. Keeping animals to be killed later is cruel. In addition, keeping animals consumes a large amount of food that could also be processed for humans. Meat is consumed by many only for taste, and it is therefore barbaric to kill other living beings for that reason.

Thefts and fraud are committed out of greed. Often, not only the loss alone, but also the fact itself has traumatic effects on the injured parties (and the perpetrator himself!). And often, not even greed is the reason for such acts, because often things are destroyed only out of hatred. The consequences are usually even worse for those affected.

Greed also has the characteristic of never really being satisfied. It constantly finds new objects that become the target of its desire.

Greed, and also hatred, are the occasions for sexual misconduct. Sexual misconduct is committed out of jealousy or pure desire. This point is not about bourgeois morals, but only about the suffering caused by such acts.

True love, which should not be confused with romantic infatuation or promises of relationships, is the basis for possible sexual connections. What many consider to be "love" is actually greed.

Basically, greed and hatred are also a form of delusion, but a very strong variant that can cause a lot of suffering.

However, delusions are all kinds of concepts and ideas that do not correspond to reality. There are many Buddhist stories about this. One of them tells of a cave dweller who sits in front of his fire and thinks the shadows on the wall are real people.

One's own experiences and the opinions of other people have provided for one's own idea of the world. Schopenhauer, a German philosopher, recognized that everyone lives in a different world despite the same environment. These are precisely the delusions that keep us from realizing the truth.

This can be seen very well even in the language: expectations (greed) are "disillusioned", after the disillusion there is no illusion, no delusion anymore (but then there are strong emotions such as hatred because one has mixed up cause and effect because of delusion).

Thich Nhat Hanh, a very honorable Vietnamese Zen master, taught to always ask if you are really sure (or subject to delusion).

A great amplifier of delusions are intoxicating substances. In the Western world, for example, alcohol is a legal intoxicant that limits one's view of reality and can promote harmful emotions.

Other intoxicants can even produce a state of consciousness that is perceived as completely real, e.g., through hallucinations.

Apart from the danger of delusions, it is extremely stupid to feed your body harmful substances. Bodo Schäfer, a German entrepreneur, once put it very nicely, saying that you wouldn't give your million-dollar racehorse hamburgers, cola and cigarettes either. So why harm yourself with something like that.

But also the consumption of certain media can lead to a distortion of reality. Not only pornography, depictions of violence, certain songs, propaganda and stories represent a false reality, but any form of dogma that creates its own reality.

Therefore, in addition to right actions, the Buddha also considers right speech to be particularly noteworthy. Through communication, whether in the media or directly, strong delusions can arise.

Lies create their own reality, which is different from the truth. Often there is damage of some kind to the person being lied to. The lie falls back on the liar, because the problem of the liar is not that no one believes him anymore, but that he does not know whom to believe.

But not only lies, such as untrue rumors, can lead to discord. The deliberate spreading of facts that unnecessarily lead to hatred and greed should also be avoided.

This also includes hurtful speech. It makes a big difference how criticism is formulated. In Japan in particular, interaction is characterized by special politeness, which is increasingly being forgotten in Western countries.

Basically, silence is preferable to senseless speech. Talking always leads to not consciously perceiving reality. Speech shapes reality into limited concepts and ideas. Meaningless chatter often leads to hurtful speech that sows discord.

The ethical principles listed above can be summarized to a certain extent with the golden rule of ethics: "Do unto others as you would have them do unto you".

Incidentally, this rule is not based on Kant's categorical imperative, but was already formulated by Confucius, later Jesus and many others. At this point, academic objections about special constellations follow, where this rule just does not apply. I like to ignore this academic arrogance.

But even better than observing ethical laws is simply to have compassion for other living beings, because all living beings want to be happy. However, it is impossible to have compassion for others if you do not have compassion for yourself.

3.3 Mindfulness and meditation: effort, mindfulness and concentration

In these indications, the Buddha wants to invite us to live a consistently mindful life and to consolidate this through practice.

Living mindfully means always being in the present. When I think about the past or the future, I cannot be in the present. When emotions are running through me because of thoughts, I am not in the present. When I think, I am not in the present. Descartes, a French philosopher and natural scientist, said "Cogito, ergo sum" (Latin: "I think, therefore I am"). He did not only deny the "being" of any kind to all those who, in his opinion, do not think, but, according to Buddhist conception, he put an essential error of thinking into the world. Only if I do not think, then I am mindful in the present. It should therefore be: "Non cogito, ergo sum" ("I do not think, therefore I am"). "Blessed are the poor in spirit", because the mind blinds reality.

Of course, this means not to never use the mind again. But the mind is only a tool that does not have to be in constant use, but is to be used to solve problems. The hammer was designed for hammering in nails. Those who constantly play around with it need not complain later when the valuable porcelain is broken when the hammer carelessly slips out of their hand.

But how do you achieve the state of present consciousness? It certainly won't work if you focus on not thinking. Try not thinking about a pink elephant playing the piano in the basement.

An introduction to the practice of meditation is to focus only on one's breathing. One consciously notices how one breathes in and out. Thoughts that inevitably arise are simply observed and not suppressed. Basically, meditation is a form of introspection. Thoughts are perceived, yet one does not identify with them. Thoughts are not needed now, yet the brain produces them incessantly, similar to faulty software.

Meditation can be practiced while sitting with the back upright. In the beginning, the practice period should not be too long. Ideally, one should set a clock to signal the expiration of the practice time. In the beginning, 5 to 10 minutes is enough. It is also better to practice several times in short intervals. Disturbing noises should also be simply observed, but not interpreted. If noises are too distracting, one could play a recording of a rushing waterfall to cover background noise. This is better than music, which may be distracting again.

You perceive how you feel your body without interpreting the stimuli that occur. The focus remains on the breathing.

One can compare the experience of meditation, the stillness of the mind, with the two states of sleeping and waking. Man is in a state of sleep, in which he dreams. When he becomes aware of the dream state, he awakens.

Meditation is like a restful dreamless sleep, but the difference is that this state is not consciously perceived during sleep.

However, it is not enough to meditate several times a day. Much more important and effective is mindfulness in everyday life. Every activity should be performed mindfully. For example, one should not be distracted by conversations while eating. When one eats, one eats. I perceive the food and reflect on the origin of my food. If you eat mindfully in this way, you can no longer eat meat, because mindfulness will inevitably lead to the memory of the suffering of the animals who had to die for this food.

Another good exercise is mindful walking. You simply put one step in front of the other and notice the feeling of walking and your surroundings. If you feel you have to evaluate anything, remind yourself to just observe it.

In the same way, all other activities are performed. Even annoying work is simply done without evaluating it. Unhappy time is lost time.

Perception should take place without the categorization into terms. If one sees a beautiful flower, one thinks neither "flower" nor "beautiful", because thereby one calls up stored patterns from the past. Only the look counts, without evaluations and descriptions. There is only perception.

Or a more practical example: You see a dog. For you, dogs are dangerous because they bark and bite. Put away the concepts and ideas, and there is only the dog and you. Now you experience the miracle of reality (dogs are, if not negatively influenced by humans, very friendly creatures that want to avoid any conflict by means of calming signals). Probably the dog will come to you and want to lick your hand as a sign of affection. As we will see later, you are mirroring each other.

However, it is as the Buddha himself put it: mindfulness and collection, that is, meditation, requires a special effort.

This does not mean the strenuous concentrated sitting in meditation, because that would make meditation wrong. Meditation is simply sitting and observing, and no concentration is required for this.

Effort means that mindfulness and collection must be performed permanently. It makes no sense to meditate briefly three times a day and then go back to daydreaming. Mindfulness must become a permanent state and to achieve this, very many years of practice are required.

The greatest difficulty lies in not being distracted by thoughts from the absolute perception of reality. "The trick is to stop thinking," as Thich Nhat Hanh said.

In Zen Buddhism, therefore, koans are used in addition to intensive meditation. A koan is a question that the master asks his student. Until he has found a solution, he is not allowed to visit the master again. If he gives a wrong answer, he will be sent away again. Only when he gives the correct answer, he receives a new koan and advances in his training.

The purpose of the koan is to confuse the mind until it finally gives up searching for a solution. Now, finally, thinking stops and an answer can be found in pure consciousness. There is no way to solve the question through logic. There is also no standardized answer. From the way the disciple answers alone, the master can tell if the answer is a real realization or just a pitiful attempt of the mind to answer.

A classic koan is "What is the sound of one hand clapping?".

Or else a story can be interpreted in the form of a koan: "To Master Joshu came a monk and asked him whether a dog has Buddha nature or not. Joshu replied: Mu!" (Meaning "Mu": Nothing there!).

The more advanced one is in meditation, the clearer an answer to these questions will be found. However, trying to find a solution by thinking will not succeed. Only when the mind stops trying, a solution will show itself.

3.4 Summary

The Noble Eightfold Path thus leads to a life of mindfulness and compassion. Through mindfulness, one comes much closer to reality than through daydreaming. This philosophy is also reflected in the widespread saying "Carpe diem" ("Pick the day") as an invitation to live in the here and now.

Adherence to the ethical principles or the golden rule leads to compassion. If these rules were observed by all people, world peace would be achieved immediately and we would live in a paradise. People on the Buddhist path ensure peace at least in their social circle.

Mindfulness and compassion, when practiced consistently as a way of life, will lead to further deep insights.

Actually, this little booklet could now end with the encouragement of unceasing practice here, because that's all you need to know about the Buddhist path.

Undoubtedly, the suffering of life is greatly reduced by following these rules.

In the Heart Sutra, however, there is an essential statement that explains the way ahead:

"Form is Emptiness, and Emptiness is Form."

Where this path leads will be explained below.

4 The Emptiness

Excerpt from the Heart Sutra:
"Form is Emptiness, and Emptiness is Form."

色不異空。空不異色。

4.1 Introduction to Emptiness

Ideally, you will already have some years of experience in mindful living when you read this chapter. It may seem very abstract to you. Don't be deterred, but continue to practice mindfulness and compassion, and question the concept of Emptiness. Because this is where it gets really exciting.

Maybe you expected something more. The ethical rules are more or less found in the laws of Western countries or in the moral code of any religion. Also the request to live in the here and now is not too new knowledge ("carpe diem!").

More interesting is already the realization that delusions prevent the view of reality. Ideas and concepts distract from reality and create a possibly painful situation.

Suffering is also created by clinging to permanence and independent existence. But is there such a thing at all?

4.2 The essence of Emptiness

In reality, there is no consistency. This is trivial and immediately obvious. Entropy means that everything strives from an ordered to a chaotic state. Buildings decay, plants wither, animals and people age, fall ill and die. The desire to hold on to a state leads to suffering, because in reality everything flows and changes.

But what about independent existence? Are there not "me" and "the others"? The individual cannot exist without his ancestors. He cannot exist without his environment. The individual is at least dependent on oxygen, water, food and energy by the sun.

Nevertheless, the individual considers himself to be something special. One sees oneself as a personality that exists separate from the rest of the world. Perhaps one sees oneself as an island in the world. Possibly one thinks of oneself as a particularly beautiful personality. The ego builds itself up on its beauty. It is far above the average of the others. The resulting delusion is nothing but arrogance, a mixture of greed (for attention) and hatred (for the inferior).

The suffering is that this independent existence does not exist. Although the expression, i.e. the form, is particularly beautiful, it is not independent of its environment, but just as dependent on it as everything else. If the environment disappears, the person also disappears (apart from that, beauty is not permanent, which immediately leads to suffering again).

Thich Nhat Hanh introduced the concept of "Interbeing" in this context. One is always part of this world, never independent.

Even in classical physics this phenomenon is known in the form of the law of conservation of energy. There is no beginning, no end and no nothing, but only change.

The model of Emptiness tries to explain this. From Emptiness arises Form, which in turn is nothing other than Emptiness.

A very good attempt at explanation is the comparison of wave and sea. The wave and the sea are the same.

Under no circumstances should Emptiness be understood as "nothingness".

Emptiness means that all Forms are empty of independent existence and permanence. Since Form and Emptiness are the same, all expressions are interconnected ("Interbeing").

The arrogant wave thinks it is more beautiful than the sea, and since it is not, it suffers. The beautiful flower will also fade in the circle of life and be part of the earth again. Because what is a "flower" in our imagination, consists in reality of non-flower parts (which are again in the natural sciences, atoms etc.).

Emptiness cannot be grasped with the mind and with concepts. The attempts to explain it are a bit like trying to describe what chocolate is. One can describe all possible facets (appearance, consistency, taste), but in the end one does not really know what chocolate is until one has tasted it oneself.

The essence of Emptiness can be grasped by switching off the mind and looking at things as they are. When concepts and ideas fall away, one can approach the essence of Emptiness. And this works only through mindful practice. The moment will come very immediately when Emptiness will be clearly revealed to you.

4.3 Consequences of Emptiness

The interconnectedness of all phenomena gives rise to consequences that extinguish all suffering.

4.3.1 Absence of an ego

In Latin, "persona" means mask. The personality or ego is nothing but a mask, that is, a delusion.

Very young children do not yet have an ego. They experience the world directly. Only through experiences, parents, educators, etc. the so-called ego is formed. Imaginations develop, which digress far from reality. If there is a discrepancy between reality and imagination, the ego suffers. Depending on the characteristics of the individual, this can lead to malice, (self-)murder and even wars. Narcissism and arrogance are a painful manifestation of the ego.

Jesus said that unless you become like children, you will not enter the Kingdom of Heaven. It is not the innocence of children propagated by the church, but the connection to their true nature, their connection to God.

If there is no ego, there is a connection between subject and object, between cause and effect. All phenomena exert a direct influence on each other. There is no separation between the individual phenomena.

The observer is the observed just as the thought is the thinker. If the thought disappears, the thinker disappears.

Physically, this can be understood, for example, in quantum mechanics as quantum entanglement.

True love does not take place in the connection of two egos, but in the connection in pure consciousness.

Animals have only a small ego, if any. They perform their actions authentically. They eat when they are hungry and sleep when they are tired. Animals are wonderful teachers.

How satisfied is a dog when he can only be with his master. Maybe he still has a small toy that contributes to his happiness, but which he does not really need.

Attentive animal husbandry means respecting the nature of an animal and not trying to change it according to one's own ideas.

With a big ego, you are like a camel that wants to go through the eye of a needle.

And there is no one independent hand which can produce a sound clapping. The conception springs from a blinded dualistic spirit. The questioner belongs to be slapped.

4.3.2 Karma

In Buddhism, there is the concept of karma. In simple words, it can be said that all one's deeds come back to oneself.

Since there is no separation of subject and object, since subject and object are the same as a Form of Emptiness, so whatever good or bad I do to others, I do to myself.

Now the ethical rules from the Noble Eightfold Path immediately become clear. Although one has not yet understood the essence of Emptiness due to lack of mindfulness, one should behave like this from now on. Every evil deed against others one does to oneself – and vice versa!

But it is the same with good deeds that you do to others, because they come back immediately. Buddhism calls this a collection of good and bad karma.

In some religions there is the postulate of charity, which seems to be difficult to fulfill.

Since subject and object are the same, the Buddha said, "You can explore the whole universe and you will not find anyone more worthy of love than yourself."

This is not a contradiction to the Christian postulate of charity, for example, but a very clear consequence of Emptiness.

Compassion for others is nothing other than compassion for oneself.

Through the equivalence of Form and Emptiness, subject and object as well as cause and effect are equivalent. Every subject is reflected in its object, but it is empty in its essence.

4.3.3 Rebirth

Although the concept of Emptiness implies rebirth (or an exit from the wheel of life), any transformation that goes beyond the conservation of energy remains a matter of faith for the one who has not grasped Emptiness.

"To be or not to be" is precisely not the question. The Form is to be questioned.

The Buddha was often asked the question of rebirth and what place his teaching has in the cycle of rebirths.

He answered with the parable of the poisoned arrow: If a poisoned arrow is stuck in the body, it does not matter at first what material it is made of, what kind of poison it contains and where it comes from. Only its removal is the only correct course of action.

First of all, the implementation of the Noble Eightfold Path must be done in order to realize the truth. All other questions are secondary and will answer themselves.

4.3.4 Connection with evil

Why is there evil in the world if everything is connected? How can you have compassion for evil people? Mu.

Or in more detail: a monk is robbed on his way to the temple (fortunately he has only his begging bowl with little alms). Once there, he angrily asks the Zen master, "Do criminals have Buddha nature?" The master replies, "Mu!"

Since everything has Form from Emptiness, of course everything has Buddha nature (even dogs – and robbers). The monk does not recognize this connection because of his dualistic attitude and asks this very nonsensical question for the master. Therefore, he answers with "Mu!", which can be translated approximately as "Nothing there!". There is nothing to affirm or to deny.

Do you have to turn the other cheek when you are beaten or even killed?
The Buddha said, "Avoid associating with fools!". However, he did not say that fools should be hated. Rather, compassion is needed for those who still suffer from delusion.

But there is nothing wrong with avoiding them. On the path, it makes sense to turn to a community of like-minded people (Sangha) rather than to deluded people.

In the universal consciousness of Emptiness there is no more dualism, no more "good and evil". It is a state of silence and unconditional love. Hate, or evil, separates us from this state.

5 Questions

The answers to these questions emerged during various retreats and Dharma talks over the course of many years.

5.1 How can you think of the world as an ocean?

The ocean consists of equal parts. Currents form in it, resulting in waves that appear individually. The currents follow a principle of creation and keep the ocean flowing. The waves have different sizes, speeds and can cancel or reinforce each other. They are not independent and not permanent, but still a part of the ocean that always exists. But the ocean is also contained in every wave, in it everything is connected.

One can imagine the waves as the individuals (lat. "indivisible") in the world, which are formed by currents. The ocean is a unity and indivisible.

5.2 Am I my body?

Possibly you are sitting on a chair right now. With the eyes of the body, thus you as subject, you regard the chair as object. In the same way, however, you can look at your legs as objects. All perceptions are transient objects. But if your body is the object, it cannot be the subject. The body is an accumulation of energy that we can observe, but to which we mistakenly habitually ascribe concepts.

5.3 Am I my mind?

Most people assume to be their mind. The subject is the mind, the thinker. Since a subject always needs an object, there are thoughts. But what happens when thoughts disappear? Then the thinker also disappears. But in the situations where one does not think, one still exists. So the thinker cannot be the subject. "I think, therefore I am", what a fallacy, because it doesn't matter whether there is thinking or not.

Thinking is an activity and not a state of being.

If you were your mind, you could predict what your next thought would be. Why don't you try it?

5.4 So what is our true existence?

So if you are neither your body nor your mind, then you would probably not exist. But you exist!

The true existence can be immediately recognized when you ask yourself the question whether you exist. The answer to this question will undoubtedly be "yes". You know that you exist, there is no doubt about it. You do not need to think about it.

But we have e.g. seen that the thinker disappears when there is no thought. The true existence exists independently of thoughts, it cannot be grasped thoughtfully at all, since it is always present. It is the all-embracing basic substance to which you belong. It is the ocean from our example. In this ocean, forms can appear, but they do not change its basic substance. We are the basic substance, but we see only the forms which are formed by currents. But if the forms disappear, the basic substance remains. We are preserved because we are the basic substance, even if our forms change or we imagine forms.

True existence is Emptiness, from which Forms can emerge. It is like a blank screen on which everything can appear.

In the cinema, we see a film that captivates us to such an extent that we no longer recognize the screen. But the film cannot harm the screen. If a house burns in the film, the screen remains. Some viewers were so blinded by a film that they shot at villains appearing there with revolvers on the screen.

True existence has no limits, it is always there. If we perceive limitations, these are merely concepts that are limited in time and space, and can therefore be processed by the mind. The true existence cannot be perceived by the mind, but we are constantly aware of it, even if delusions distract us temporarily. Thus, the question of being or non-being is also an illusion.

By staying in the present, we are in contact with the true nature. The ego exists only in thoughts in the past and future. In our true nature we are connected with everything ("Interbeing").

Being is unconditional. We may reject forms of existence, but they are merely forms that we do not like. Unfortunately for our ego, we do not have too much influence on the currents that create these forms. But since evaluation and rejection are illusions, true existence is unconditional and cannot be other than accepted. Acceptance, however, is nothing else than love, thus our true existence is nothing else than unconditional love. Since this has always been so, one can also experience all resistances more calmly.

Body and mind are objects that can be perceived. They are perceived within our true existence. Only these objects can be experienced as form, but they are limited in time and space. The empty true existence is unlimited and not graspable, but we are always aware of it. It does not end with death, that is, the end of the body and the mind.

Unfortunately, only a few scientists undertake the research of near-death experiences. During the time of near-death, brain waves are no longer measurable, so the person is dead. After some time, however, it is possible to reanimate the patient. Some patients report their experiences during this time. They can see their body from the outside, and hear what is spoken. This is not a dream state, as brain waves can no longer be measured. Very often a very bright light appears, which is perceived as unconditional love and which attracts one. The return to the physical state is then often perceived as very unpleasant, often with the condition that one is not yet ready for the new state.

These patients have experienced that there is an infinite true existence. Unfortunately, these results are rejected by a large part of science.

5.5 What is the ego?

The ego is an illusory mental concept that sees itself as the subject for the perception of all objects. If a new object appears in its field of vision, it is immediately categorized and identified with it. This is very convenient for the ego, since this dualistic categorization gives an illusion of security and seems to explain the world easily.

Time is another important factor for the ego. It does not like to dwell in the now. It is only through the definition of time that the illusion of permanence and independent existence is created. With deep looking, however, one realizes that in fact there is not a constant feeling of ego. Thus, the ego thought is just as fleeting as any other. The only time that really exists is the present moment. Everything else is past or future, that is, illusion.

Whenever we are in the past or in the future in our thoughts, the ego has superimposed itself on our pure consciousness and we have lost contact with our true existence. Therefore, it is important to stay in the present in meditation. The flow of thoughts dries up, silence returns and we are connected with our true nature.

The ego craves opposites to maintain the sense of separation from objects without it cannot exist.

But since the ego is only a thought, it can also only recognize other thoughts. Our true existence, however, is beyond fleeting thoughts and thus cannot be recognized by the ego thought. Thus, if we seek our true existence with the help of the ego, we are like the seeker of the gateless gate. The gate to our true existence is always there, but it is not recognized because it is sought as a gate. If the ego thought disappears, the thought of a gate disappears and it can be passed through. The Buddha nature has been recognized.

If the belief in an ego ends, one recognizes its true existence, beyond space and time, concepts and ideas.

5.6 How do I live without ego?

In Zen Buddhism, there is a statement that a mountain becomes a non-mountain and then becomes a mountain again. So only the point of view changes.

Life continues to flow normally, as it did before. Only attachments and illusions are missing.

The elimination of the belief in an ego sometimes leads to spontaneous serenity, because one has seen through the illusion.

Feelings will still occur, but the identification with them will fall away. Learned abilities will remain, because they already existed during the time of the ego illusion, but perhaps new perspectives will arise, because one is no longer attached to concepts.

Suffering no longer becomes attachment because one does not identify with it. Letting go eliminates suffering.

A supreme expression of this letting go is the Christian cross. Despite the torture, Jesus said, "Thy will be done".

Letting go means to move out in the flow of energy instead of offering resistance. Martial arts such as Aikido or the principle of "Wuwei" (non-action against nature) are based on this principle.

The karmic cycle of action and reaction is broken.

However, letting go or surrendering does not mean giving up. Only no more resistive valuation occurs. Action is taken in the present moment and a solution is found.

Only an unconscious person can be manipulated and exploited. Just don't play the game of unconscious people anymore. Don't judge and fight them, have compassion for them, and, in the last consequence, avoid dealing with them.

5.6.1 Perception

Perception or consciousness as interface changes without the filtering by an ego.

Without the subject-object relation there is only the activity of seeing. Nothing is packed into terms anymore, put into relation, compared and evaluated. If you look at a a flower, only the activity of seeing happens. There is no evaluation there and also no attachment. The egoless mind only looks, it does not pick.

Viewer and the viewed become one. If the seer falls away, the seen is also gone, because the activity is missing. Everything else is conception.

Even if parts of the perception fall away, we are still aware of our existence.

5.6.2 Problems

If the ego thought tries to solve problems, it can only do so with the help of thoughts from the past. However, a thought cannot go beyond itself and thus a conflict arises, which only intensifies the problem and causes separation.

If the problem is considered without ego thoughts, the solution is also found within the problem. Genius discoveries of mankind have only been made this way. The nondual problem solution avoids the mistake, of which Karl Jaspers already spoke in the subject-object split.

5.6.3 Fear

Fears are thoughts about non-existent events from the future. If you look deeply, you can see that fear is merely an energy that has been given concepts. If one removes these concepts ("fear", "oppressive feeling" etc.), this energy changes and continues to flow. Letting go liberates from fear and suffering.

Fears exist in thoughts of the past or future. In the present there are no thoughts and therefore no fear.

This excludes fear as a survival reflex, of course, but not the majority of imagined fears.

5.7 Form is Emptiness is Form?

Form is Emptiness – Forms, especially the ego, are empty of permanence and independent existence.

Emptiness is Form – the true existence is neither only Form nor object, and therefore unattainable for thoughts, it appears empty. But because of this Emptiness, it can make all Forms appear and disappear.

5.8 Is life really nondual?

True existence is indeed nondual, as we have seen. The duality of our world arises primarily from language, which works with subjects and objects. From this, terms are then derived, which in turn are categorized, as they make life easier.

Children and animals experience the world nondually. It is only when you teach children language that their perspective changes.

Language is not only a tool for communication, but a perfect means for manipulation.

The truth is nondual and can only be recognized without the filter of an evaluating ego. The true existence is always present, in it limited dualistic concepts rise. When these are recognized, identification and attachment no longer occur.

Subject and object are part of dualism. But subject and object are in truth empty and mirror each other. The subject is in the object, and vice versa, both are empty. We are connected to everything. We are a unity in Emptiness and therefore at the same time mirroring in Form. The form is also empty. It's more than connection, it's Interbeing.

5.9 What does Satori look like?

When I finally arrived at the statue of Hachiko at Shibuya Station in Tokyo, I wanted to be happy. I finally saw a picture of this faithful dog who had waited in vain for 11 years for his master to arrive at the station because he could not understand that he had died. Hachiko lived unconditional love. Even during his lifetime, the Japanese were so enthusiastic that they built a statue of him. This was later sacrificed for a terrible war, but fortunately was rebuilt a few years later. I finally wanted to see this symbol of unconditional love and peace.

Once there, there was loud chaos. Located on the busy Yamanote Line, Shibuya Station is a hub not far from the busiest station in the world, Shinjuku eki. The statue of Hachiko is a popular meeting place for those meeting in Shibuya.

At the time I arrived there, it was evening rush hour. Next to the Hachiko statue, a black van with oversized loudspeakers had lined up, barking nationalist slogans into the area. There was no place to look at Hachiko in peace. I was sorely disappointed, all my beautiful expectations were gone. Here I stood, and far away Hachiko. I just wanted to leave.

At that moment the situation changed. The noise became a background noise, the many people were still there, but I perceived them as energy fields similar to a thermal imaging camera. Time seemed to stand still, it was just one big room. I no longer felt any separation between me and everything. Everything was the same, there was no more attachment, only perceptions.

I don't know how long I stayed there, but even when I left, the mass of people and noise no longer bothered me.

The state slowly faded away, but this experience once seen, this sudden change of consciousness, could not be erased. It's like realizing that a dangerous snake was just a rope. Never again will one mistake the rope for a snake. The gateless gate had been passed through.

Of course, the ego kept coming back, but it was recognized as an illusion and no longer believed. When I experienced myself far from this state, meditations led me back again.

6 Final Consideration

So far we have perceived ourselves as a person/ego with characteristics, past and future plans. However, we could not answer simple questions whether we are our body (carrier) or mind (tool). Body we cannot be, because we can perceive ourselves as object with our eyes. Also we cannot be the mind, because there are phases without thoughts and we do not disappear. Even our next thought we cannot predict. So we should not exist at all, but we are nevertheless conscious of our existence.

In this respect our idea of us as a person/ego is an illusion we believe when we are not present. We can just as well give up this belief and continue to live within the framework of our true existence, because we have always done it this way, even if we didn't realize it. The ego has blinded us too much, we no longer had a connection to our true existence.

The true existence is Emptiness, which appears as illusionary Form.

This unconditional loving true existence has always carried us. The fuss with the ego was unnecessary. From now on, we can enjoy life much more serenely in the moment. Suffering is over.

Buddhism helps us understand this concept with its model of Emptiness. We perceived ourselves as form, although at the same time we are emptiness. Even more, we are emptiness as our true existence. Creative currents designed forms with which we identified and constructed a story according to our ego conceptions. We were very afraid that we would disappear with the dissolution of the form, but we only change, because we can let all forms appear in us as emptiness. There are limits to our creativity insofar as we can influence the principles of the currents that create the forms only to certain extends.

Possibly, without the emptiness model of Buddhism, we would not have come to this understanding. For this we thank the many Buddhas who prepared the way to this realization for us. Nevertheless, it is very exhilarating to see how simple questions can be used to fathom the answer to our true existence.

If one had recognized this shortcut a little earlier, one could perhaps have spared oneself the years of expectant sitting in Zen. Simply sitting would have been enough.

7 Summary

Four Noble Truths:

1. life is suffering
2. causes of suffering are unwholesome actions
3. abolition of suffering through avoidance of unwholesome actions
4. the way is the Noble Eightfold Path

The Noble Eightfold Path:

1. right view, right thought

realization and decision for the path of the Buddha

2. right action, right speech and right livelihood

avoidance of unwholesome actions:

- three basic poisons: delusion, greed and hatred
- killing, stealing, sexual misconduct, consumption of mental poisons
- lying, hurtful speech, sowing discord, senseless chatter

3. right effort, right mindfulness, right concentration

living in the present consciousness

- meditation in breathing, walking and eating, and mindful practice

- mindfulness (to recognize reality) and compassion (happiness of all living beings)

Emptiness:

- suffering is clinging to permanence and independent existence as well as ideas and concepts
- Form is Emptiness and Emptiness is Form
- empty of constancy and independence, Interbeing
- there is no ego
- equality of object and subject, cause and effect
- karma: everything you do to others you do to yourself
- avoid dealing with fools, but have compassion

Questions:

- ocean, waves and currents are one unit
- body and mind are objects
- one is undoubtedly aware of the true existence, it is unconditional love
- with the removal of belief in an ego, one approaches Satori
- in thought in the past and future is the state of the ego
- dwelling in the present is silence, our true nature
- all sense impressions are activities, consciousness happens directly, value-free and without attachment
- the answer of the problem is in the problem
- fears are blocked energies, in the present there are no thoughts and therefore no fear
- subject and object are empty and mirror each other, connected in Emptiness, one unity, Interbeing

- the true existence is neither only Form nor object, inaccessible to mind, it can make everything appear because of the Emptiness

Conclusion:

- we are not body (carrier) or mind (tool)
- we exist even when the mind stops and cannot predict thoughts
- the ego disappears when we are present
- true existence is Emptiness, which appears as illusionary Form

Living a Buddhist life:

- living in mindfulness and compassion
- no unwholesome actions
- efficient mind
- feelings without identification and attachment
- no fear of death
- living in the present
- direct perception of the world
- trust in life (Wuwei)
- living in unconditional love in unity of life (or God)

8 References

Borg, Jesus and Buddha

Brunnhölzl, The Heart Attack Sutra

Bukkyo Dendo Kyokai, The Teaching of Buddha

Cairns, For The Love Of Everything

Dalai Lama, How to See Yourself As You Really Are

Dalai Lama, The Four Noble Truths

Deshimaru-Roshi, Za-Zen

Haduch, Form is… Emptiness …is Form

Henriksson, The Secret Book of Zen

Kyhentse, What Makes You Not a Buddhist

Long, Evidence of the Afterlife. The Science of Near-Death Experience

Mingyur Rinpoche, The Joy of Living: Unlocking the Secret and Science of Happiness

Moody, Life After Life

Mumon, The Gateless Gate

Nishijima, To meet the real dragon

Osho, Awareness

Osho, Beyond the Frontier of the Mind

Sekida, Zen Training

Sheng Yen, There is no suffering

Suzuki, Zen Mind, Beginner's Mind

Thich Nhat Hanh, Buddha Mind, Buddha Body: Walking Toward Enlightenment

Thich Nhat Hanh, Going Home. Jesus and Buddha as Brothers

Thich Nhat Hanh, Nothing to do – Nowhere to go

Thich Nhat Hanh, The Diamond That Cuts Through Illusion

Thich Nhat Hanh, The Heart of the Buddha's Teaching

Thich Nhat Hanh, The Heart of Understanding: A New Translation of the Heart Sutra with Commentaries

Thich Nhat Hanh, Opening the Heart of the Cosmos. Insights on the Lotos Sutra

Thich Nhat Hanh, Zen Battles

Thich Nhat Hanh, Zen Keys

Tolle, The Power Of Now

Tolle, A New Earth

Uchiyama Roshi, Reality of Zazen

Warner, Hardcore Zen

Wright, Why Buddhism Is True

Satori

Not body, not mind

Predict your thought, impossible

Do you exist?

Stop thinking, ego thinker vanishes

Perceive directly in awareness

From Emptiness, unconditional love, formed by creational
currents

You are Form, empty from permanent and independent ego

In Interbeing in Emptiness

Illusionary Form dissolves